A Best of
Creative Training Techniques Newsletter Book

P9-EMN-514

MANAGING
THE FRONT-END
OF TRAINING

101

Ways to

Analyze

Training Needs —

And Get Results

■ ■ ■

By Bob Pike with Chris Busse

Lakewood Publications
A Maclean Hunter Company

Quantity Sales

Most Lakewood books are available at special quantity discounts when purchased in bulk by companies, organizations and special-interest groups. Custom imprinting or excerpting can also be done to fit special needs. For details contact Lakewood Books.

■ ■ ■

LAKEWOOD BOOKS

50 South Ninth Street
Minneapolis, MN 55402
(800) 707-7769 or (612) 333-0471
FAX (612) 340-4819

Publisher: Philip G. Jones
Editors: Bob Pike with Julie Tilka
Production Editor: Julie Tilka
Production: Carol Swanson and Pat Grawert
Cover Designer: Barb Betz, Betz Design

10 9 8 7 6 5 4 3 2 1

Lakewood Publications, Inc. publishes *TRAINING Magazine; Training Directors' Forum Newsletter; Creative Training Techniques Newsletter; Technology For Learning Newsletter; Potentials In Marketing* Magazine, *Presentations* Magazine; and other business periodicals, books, research and conferences.

Bob Pike, Creative Training Techniques International, 7620 W. 78th St., Edina, MN 55439, (612) 829-1960, FAX (612) 829-0260.

ISBN 0-943210-67-4

Contents

Foreword

This book, *Managing the Front-End of Training*, is one in a series drawn from the best content of *Creative Training Techniques Newsletter*. The newsletter was conceived in 1988 by editor and internationally known trainer Bob Pike to be a one-stop resource of practical "how-tos" for trainers. The idea was (and still is) to provide timely tips, techniques, and strategies that help trainers with the special tasks they perform daily.

When the newsletter began, it was largely fueled by Bob's 20 years of experience in the field and by the best ideas shared by the trainers (more than 15,000 in all) who had attended his Creative Training Techniques seminars. As the newsletter grew in popularity, it also began to draw on ideas submitted by its readers. Today, the newsletter continues to search out creative approaches from the more than 200 seminars Bob and the other Creative Training Techniques trainers conduct every year, and from the newsletter readers.

But no matter where the insights come from, the goal of the newsletter remains the same: To provide trainers a cafeteria of ideas they can quickly absorb, and then choose those that best suit their special needs.

This series of books represents the best ideas from *Creative Training Techniques Newsletter's* six years of publication. It is our hope we've created a valuable resource you'll come back to again and again to help address the unique challenges you face in your job every day.

Sincerely,
The Editors

Introduction

Every trainer has heard it at one point or another: A manager talks with you about the possibility of a training session, and when you ask the manager when he or she would like to have the course ready to go, the answer is "Yesterday."

Shrinking the time that elapses between identifying a training need and delivering a program has always been crucial for technical audiences, where state-of-the-art work systems and technology can change with alarming speed. But in the wake of downsizing and work reengineering trends, the demand for customized, "just-in-time" training has spread to the general employee population as well.

These are things that we are concerned with right now, but the effective design and delivery of training has always been important. Any good design begins with a needs assessment and front-end analysis that is proactive rather than reactive. Too often, a needs assessment has consisted of a manager simply saying, for example, "We need a stress management assessment," rather than formally identifying the performance gap between high and low performers that can be closed by an effective training program.

The dilemma of all these trends is clear: Training programs can seriously suffer from a lack of preparation (which includes an effective needs assessment), yet there is less and less preparation time being built into the process for courses that are asked to be more and more job-specific.

An informal survey conducted by *Training Directors' Forum Newsletter* highlights the bind in which many trainers find themselves. It discovered that nearly all respondents agree a trend toward more specialized training exists, and that there's a demand for that specialized material to be delivered as "just-in-time" training. But only half say the demand for that kind of training, deliverable on relatively short notice, is one they're able to meet.

In the best of all possible worlds, you would, of course, have ample time to conduct a formal needs analysis and pay close attention to the small, administrative details necessary to get a course up and running. In reality, however, that doesn't always happen. Yes, good training can take place with a minimum of front-end preparation, but adequate preparation can often mean the difference between a good session and a great one.

That's where *Managing the Front-End of Training* can help. The ideas in this book are designed to help you conduct quick, accurate needs assessments of your target audiences and to start thinking about the logistical details that will ultimately make any session a success. Reading these ideas and working to stay ahead of those front-end challenges — regardless of the type of training you'll deliver — will enable you to present courses that will delight your training customers and make a difference in your organization.

Bob Pike

Section One:
Administration Tips

The beginning of some programs can be sluggish due to an abundance of necessary, but dull, administrative details. Victoria Dietrich, manager of human resource development for the Chicago Mercantile Exchange, avoids slow starts by holding orientation meetings *before* any training series for her organization.

At the meeting, she introduces her objectives, helps people get acquainted with one another and the materials, and begins to develop groups that will be used during training.

Dietrich's strategy eliminates a major problem that occurs when the first 30 to 60 minutes of the first class is devoted to an orientation. When people have to shift from gathering information to becoming active participants, the class often gets off to a slow start.

Dietrich's idea makes the first day of training a truly active one. The group feels mentally prepared to learn, and has already begun to form relationships.

1

Address details before training to avoid a slow start

2

Directory listing subject-matter experts is valued resource

A human resource directory created by Brian Moffitt, staff development coordinator at San Diego Mental Health Services, helps employees make maximum use of people in their organizations who are subject-matter experts (SMEs).

The experts are listed according to subject matter, specific availability, and method of information sharing preferred. The directory is published twice yearly and is updated as needed. Moffitt's department provides incentives for those who participate as SMEs.

Elizabeth Jeffries, a Louisville, KY-based training consultant, always solicits input from as many participants as she has time for before finalizing plans for a seminar. She calls them to ask what they're expecting, the challenges of their jobs, and so on.

She then uses some of the comments (with permission of the participants) during her presentation. It adds credibility to the seminar because people realize she takes the time to do her homework.

3

Solicit participant input before designing programs

4

Managers help to 'close the training loop'

Lea Buikstra, a trainer for Store Cable Communications, reviews the objectives of a training course with company managers prior to presenting the course. That session is followed by a "closure" program after the course.

Participants are certified for completing the program and receive diplomas only after they have "closed the loop." Their supervisors get a list of skills and tasks learned, and must witness the employees demonstrating them on the job to ensure training has transferred.

Reduce the anxiety line managers feel about participating in an upcoming seminar by providing as much preparation material as possible, says Phil Cowan, training and development manager for Pick 'n Save, a national retailer.

"A no-surprise package works best," he says. "Provide as much information up front as you can. Let them know exactly what they'll be doing. The more prereading they have, the more receptive they're likely to be in the seminar.

"Many managers see training as having to leave major responsibilities, being pulled away from family, and having to sit there bored for three days. So if you get them to come in motivated, there's a much better chance the session will be successful."

Cowan sends prep materials six weeks before the seminar so managers have plenty of time to review them and follow up. "It gives them a chance to get back to you and say, 'Hey, you sent an article on what's being covered, but can I get more reading material?'"

A strong emphasis on seminar preparation, Cowan believes, makes people ready to share information.

5

Giving managers ample prep time reduces anxieties

6

Organizing handouts by color makes them user-friendly

Preparing handouts with page numbers and differentiating subjects by paper color makes it easier for participants to get organized and stay organized, says St. Paul, MN-based consultant Marjorie Pabst. Participants can then refer to and review the material by page number. And because each topic has a different color it's quick and easy to locate appropriate material.

When you change small-group composition frequently, Robin Vinden of Bell Canada suggests preparing a name tag system that gives you a number of easy options to reorganize groups.

Different colored name tags designate the first breakouts. Before passing them out, she places a number at the lower left corner of each tag to create new teams. She asks people to realign themselves by number, and later asks them to create teams where all numbers are different. Vinden also places various symbols in the lower right corner to realign teams in that manner.

7

Name tag coding system makes rearranging groups easy

8

Keep close tabs on handouts susceptible to change

One of the dilemmas trainers face is keeping handouts and exercises current, particularly those that are price-sensitive or form-based. A price change or form revision means you must remember all the lessons that such modifications affect, dig through piles of material, and make the necessary corrections.

Bob Tomayko, sales training specialist for Tom's Foods Inc., has successfully addressed this issue. He keeps a master file of all the handouts and exercises needed for courses in notebooks with clear sheet protectors and places a large, red Day-Glo sticker on the protector if the handout is affected by price and a yellow sticker if it's form sensitive.

Tomayko says the stickers are big enough to write on, and he can list the particular form that's used in each exercise. That way he can update materials when a change occurs or at least know which ones to check before running copies for classroom work.

The manager registered for your program is not always the person you need to connect with in the weeks before the course. In many cases, addressing your correspondence to an administrative support person more likely ensures that your participants will arrive prepared for the course.

David Hardison, a vice president at HCA Management Co., asks people as they register for his courses if they want to include the name of a support person. Then almost all correspondence, whether by mail or by phone, goes through that assistant.

9

Send vital material to support staff of management trainees

10

Preclass surveys identify unique needs of incoming classes

Every new group of participants brings a distinct set of needs to the classroom, so Bob Hunter, a trainer with Jostens in Minneapolis, makes sure he has a good grasp of those needs before class ever begins. He sends prework questionnaires to all participants before his customer service training sessions, then uses their responses to tailor content where needed.

Some of the fill-in-the-blank questions Hunter sends to trainees — most of whom are customer service representatives — include:

Pre-Work Questionnaire Sample

• The people and events that increase demand (stress) on me in my role as a customer service representative are

---

• I know when I'm overstressed because (my early warning signals are)

• The most difficult part of dealing with internal or external customers over the phone is

---

• I feel most customer service representatives could improve their skills in these areas:

• I will consider this program worthwhile if

Fielding an onslaught of participant questions can often throw a course seriously off schedule. In classes Beth Schmidt teaches managers on improving face-to-face communication skills with subordinates, she gets a host of questions about peripheral communication topics such as listening skills, conducting meetings, or public speaking.

To avoid lengthy question-and-answer sessions, Schmidt, an editor with the Public Service Co. of Oklahoma, Tulsa, created a handout listing 30 additional resources available in her company on improving communication skills — including books, audiocassettes, videos, and related training classes.

"It allows me to stay focused on the topic at hand and provide a valuable resource tool at the same time," Schmidt says.

11

All-inclusive resource limits time-consuming questions

12

Simplest planning details can make or break a program

Factors that can make or break a program are frequently the simplest ones. Getting participants and speakers together in a room can seem like an incredibly complicated process. Your speaker's message may be timely and inspiring, your participants eager and anxious to learn, but before any of the magic you hope for takes place you have to make sure you're on top of the details that can sometimes make or break a program.

Before the program:

• Send a detailed cover letter along with your signed contract to the hotel or conference center that explains exactly what you expect from its staff.

• Make sure the hotel staff knows there shouldn't be constant interruptions, that phone calls should be held and so on.

• Designate a person on the staff who your speaker can contact if problems with the room arise.

• Send copies of the agreement made with the facility to the speaker and other program staff.

• Ship materials to the meeting site to a specific person in the hotel and clearly label each box.

• Have your speaker check room set-up and audiovisual equipment before the program begins.

During the program:

• Use real coffee cups instead of Styrofoam, and glasses instead of disposable cups.

• Provide a pad and pencil for each participant.

• Use a coffee break alternative; try Popsicles or frozen fruit juice bars.

• Serve lighter lunches and skip desserts to help participants from getting sleepy.

• Provide nonalcoholic beverage alternatives at receptions.

• Create opportunities for people to mix and allow adequate break time for renewing friendships and informal networking.

• Use variety in your room set-ups. If you have a two-day program, for instance, try using banquet-style round tables one day and herring-bone 6 foot x 30 inch (or 18 inch) tables the next.

• Have speakers available for informal discussions and functions, such as right after the presentation and during social hours and meals.

• Have your program location compatible with your objectives. Don't schedule meetings for 16 hours a day in a resort setting or for four hours a day where there are no other activities available.

13

Signs that point the way to class set a helpful tone

Be generous with directional signs that help people find their way to the training room, says Bibi Runyan, records analyst for the Workers Compensation Board in Toronto. Start with a sign outside your room, make additional signs to post as you work your way back, past elevators and all key turning points en route, to the front lobby of the hotel or convention center. Runyan points out that if people get lost trying to locate the room they may arrive feeling frustrated or embarrassed and unready to participate.

Evaluate whether the paper color, texture, and colored inks for the printed material sent from your department are being used to their best advantage to convey the appropriate message. Here are two ideas that may help get your literature noticed:

• Donna Maxon, manager of operations training for Citibank, puts pizzazz in her communications by using a custom letterhead made up with the words "Training Bulletin" printed in purple and blue on ivory linen-textured paper. She reports it motivates people to take note of the bulletin and to save it since the look and feel conveys a sense of quality and importance.

• Judy Sensabaugh, training coordinator for the Amoco Research Center, goes for optimum visibility by printing course announcements on Day-Glo copy paper — chartreuse and shocking pink seem to really stand out. Even people who get mountains of mail can't help noticing her course announcements.

14

Design bulletins to stand apart in a mountain of mail

15

Outside experts can provide fresh ideas to courses

It is helpful to have people who don't design, deliver, or manage training involved in the training and development process.

• Katie Silva, assistant vice president of Boatman's Bancshares, recommends "getting your experts involved." As course material is being developed, she has the material sent out to eight or nine people selected for their subject-matter expertise and for their positions of influence in the organization. The experts review the material to make sure the course being developed is on target. Silva is then assured the program's content is on track and has a board of advisors and subject-matter experts who help market the course and add credibility.

• Amoco Research Center has established "education coordinator" positions within each operating company at its research facility in Naperville, IL. Those individuals coordinate and develop technical training programs of particular interest to their respective companies. Each program utilizes a committee of internal experts, usually practitioners and subject-matter experts, to define course requirements and objectives.

Richard Urisko, senior manager of personnel at Hitachi America Limited, has an effective way of developing critical incidents to use in training and in a newsletter he distributes to participants. He follows up one month after each training program with a letter asking each participant to "tell a story" about how the training proved effective. Urisko publishes the stories he receives in the newsletter. The strategy reinforces the training for participants and develops ongoing interest in the course for people yet to take it. Additionally, the recognition of seeing their names in print rewards people for applying course content back on the job.

16

Follow-up newsletter is eye-catching marketing tool

17

Traveling trainers: Keep resources at your fingertips

The more information she has at her fingertips, the less time she wastes getting prepared and the more time she has to perfect her presentations, says René Besold, assistant director to education and research at the California School Employees' Association in San Jose, CA.

As a multiple locale trainer, Besold says, it is crucial to be organized. For last-minute supplies in the location where she is set to train, she keeps a listing of materials suppliers in her calendar/telephone index, filed alphabetically by city. For example:

Denver:
- Copies/faxes: Copymat 555-1234
  10¢/page $1/page
- Flip-chart paper: Robert's Supply
  555-3344
  $11/3 pads
- Markers/tape: Jason's Office
  Supply 555-9876

Lisa Miley, office automation specialist for the Florida department of education, has cut down on no-shows and cancellations by sending a follow-up letter of confirmation immediately after someone signs up for training. One week before training the registration is reconfirmed and the day before the course starts a phone call is made to remind each participant of his or her commitment.

18

Reduce no-shows with follow-up call and letter

19

Create a list of 'hot potential' trainees

As you conduct a variety of training programs, tell participants of upcoming programs and collect the names and telephone numbers of people who are interested in attending. This tactic gives you a list of "hot potential" candidates for specific mailings or publicity.

If you charge back for training, then a related tactic used by Sandy Wilson, a Mill Creek, WA, consultant, may work for you. Two to three weeks before a class is scheduled to start, ask if a participant will trade tuition for making a call to everyone on your "hot potential" list for that seminar.

20

Computer software improves training administration

Charles Bicknell, vice president and corporate training manager at Home Savings of America, suggests these two ways to use the computer to help improve administration:

1. Evaluation of training programs.

Problem: Manual process of collecting, analyzing and evaluating data for training programs is time consuming and cumbersome.

Solution: Collect data from pre- and post-course evaluations so it can be expressed numerically and placed in a database. Then data can be used to create charts to show highs, lows, and averages. Data for different courses also can be compared and analyzed.

2. Determining the quality of outside training.

Problem: It's difficult for trainees to know the quality of outside courses.

Solution: Set up a database of all outside courses used by other employees and include their evaluations. Give prospective attendees access to the database when they consider a particular course, then add their evaluations to the database when they finish the course.

21

Information 'reminder' cards eliminate last-minute hassles

Carolyn Balling, a California-based consultant, recommends this idea for trainers who travel extensively. Write all information you need regarding the site, contacts, emergency contacts, phone numbers, etc. on small, wallet-sized cards encased in plastic sleeves. Balling says the little time it takes to fill out the cards virtually eliminates hassles in personal organization when you can least afford the time.

Sometimes it's tough to decide when to distribute handouts or when to give participants more note paper. One solution is to bind all handouts into one booklet or insert them into a three-ring binder. If they're bound, intersperse blank pages so participants find convenient notepaper when a subject is discussed. If a three-ring notebook is used, simply supply blank sheets at the back of the binder, where they can be removed and inserted as desired throughout the session.

When a small quantity of handouts doesn't seem to warrant binding or a special notebook, leave several inches of blank space on each handout, either at the bottom or along one side. Provide extra blank sheets that participants can pick up as needed.

22

Binding handouts cuts distribution time

23

File folders simplify organizing preclass materials

A simple way to keep an individual participant's preclass materials organized is to label a file folder for each participant while preparing a program. All information that typically is distributed when the class begins can conveniently be placed in each individual's file.

At registration time, give each participant the folder you have prepared. As the class progresses they can add additional class notes and materials to the folder. It's a quick, efficient way to manage miscellaneous materials and keep each trainee's papers together and confidential.

24

Beware of yellow highlighters on photocopied materials

Warning: Heavy yellow highlighting can make a photocopy look like "a Watergate transcript," in the words of Peter Gradey, a training group leader for the California Employment Development Department. If you or your participants plan to make copies of notes that are highlighted, use light blue highlighters for best results. When yellow highlighting is copied, the material can end up being deleted because the machine reproduces it as gray or black.

Likewise, bright yellow or "goldenrod" paper is great for attracting attention but reserve it for "throwaway" announcements and notices, don't use it for information that a participant might want to photocopy.

25

Promotional notices have greatest impact in unusual places

Do you want to inexpensively and effectively promote your programs? Consider this idea from Jackie Wallis, education specialist at Lakeland Regional Medical Center. Wallis places 10 promotional cards in the Lakeland cafeteria advertising upcoming courses, and three more printed notices in stalls of various restrooms throughout the medical center. These are locations Wallis believes people have both the "downtime" and inclination to read such promotions.

A little personalization can go a long way toward making participants feel welcome in a training class, says Bridgette Robinson, training manager for the U.S. Postal Service. She writes a short personal note on the form letter sent to all of her participants. The notes often say something like, "Looking forward to seeing you, Betty, at the upcoming training session." That small effort does more than many trainers know to personalize the invitation, and has the trainees looking with anticipation toward the session.

26

Personalized invitations set the mood for upcoming training

27

To boost credibility, have someone introduce you

Give yourself the introduction you deserve. Too often in training programs, particularly corporate training programs, trainers — usually out of modesty — don't do enough to let their participants know just how credible they are. Next time you hold a training program for more than a dozen people, arrange for someone to introduce you, sharing with participants your credibility, your experience, and what you bring to the training program. It sets an upbeat tone for the course, and provides the trainer with some "warm fuzzies" as an energizer at the beginning of a program.

Clever posters give low-response programs a boost

When response to training is less than enthusiastic, it may be time for a promotional plan. Joan Senitz, a personnel officer with the city of Phoenix, hired a training professional to conduct and market training but still did not get much response or enthusiasm for city programs.

Her solution was a three-week ad campaign that brought strong results. The first week she posted signs with the statement, "It's Coming." A week later she posted new signs reading: "It's Almost Here." The following week she hung posters reading: "Here It Is!" with attached flyers in bright colors detailing the training calendar for two months. Concurrent with the posters she mailed the same calendars to all employees in five different colors to test which colors were more effective.

Senitz reports registration response to the classes was excellent.

29

Pre-course information reassures students class logistics are carefully planned

Even if some of your participants are familiar with how your courses run, and when and where they are located, it reassures participants when they know class logistics have been carefully planned.

With that in mind, Ion Cocks, training consultant with Employment and Immigration Canada, sends out complete instructions two or three weeks prior to his courses. His mailing includes course location, a list of those attending, a map and travel instructions from major transportation terminals, and pre-course materials or special instructions. It increases the comfort level of all participants.

A related note: Sandy Austin, an education specialist for the Bureau of Land Management, recognizes that not all participants want their names and addresses given out. She waits until the beginning of the session and then passes a sign-up sheet among participants and asks those who want their names distributed to sign their names and their phone numbers. Before the session ends she makes copies for everybody and distributes them. It's a useful networking and resource tool.

Publicizing in-house training videos can boost their usage — and the training budget. Bill Kramer, a training supervisor at IMT Fertilizer Inc., has dramatically increased the use of audiovisual materials in his training department, and as a result, increased his audiovisual budget.

Kramer now publishes and distributes an annual audiovisual catalog that has more than 900 listings, mainly videotapes available to his department. The compilation of audiovisual resources has made it easier for the company's managers and supervisors to request the materials for use in their own meetings. And that heavy usage is negotiating fodder when training's audiovisual budget is considered, says Kramer.

A similar strategy may be effective for lists of training books on specific topics, or consultants upon whom trainers or managers may want to draw to improve their department's effectiveness.

30

Publicizing training videos can increase usage, budget

31

Checklists for off-site training minimize errors

Developing a checklist to account for every possible item you need for a particular training program will ensure you'll always have everything you need. To be more useful, the checklist should be revised and improved after each time it's used.

The checklist should include everything from a knife to open boxes, to the tape to reseal the boxes of leftover materials, to the proper kind of marker to print name tags or name tents, and any collateral materials needed such as puzzles, dominoes, or game pieces. List absolutely anything you need to make sure the program goes smoothly. If you have others helping you, you can add a measure of accountability by putting initials next to each item as it is packed.

32

Executive briefings can help improve support for training

A "Founder's Workshop" or executive briefing can increase buy-in and support for your training programs. The idea is to provide a meeting for managers who need to be informed about training but have time constraints or who simply have no need to attend an entire program.

Lynn Sweet of Craftmart holds these workshops for key managers and supervisors. The workshops give them a bird's-eye view of the programs that have been developed, with key results and topics included. Attendees get special recognition and pins indicating their part as founders in creating and making these programs available. Line buy-in for the programs is much easier when participants realize and see firsthand the management support behind the program.

33

Enlisting a 'volunteer aide' helps trainers focus on content

To help your next training program go more smoothly, ask for a volunteer from the group to assume responsibility for signing people in, checking coffee breaks, working the film projector, turning lights on and off as necessary, and other administrative details. This frees you to focus on content and participant inquiries. Make sure the volunteer receives some reward of your choosing at the end of the class.

There may be times when a U-shape class arrangement serves your needs — especially if you have 10 or 15 participants. Try this arrangement: Place the 10 or 15 chairs on the outside of the U, and add five unused chairs on the inside. Small subgroups that face each other can be quickly formed by moving five participants to the empty chairs for the activity. When the activity is over participants can return to their original seats.

34

U-shape is flexible seating arrangement

35

Newsprint stretches your training budget

Becky Bowman of the Clarke County Board of Commissioners, Athens, GA, stretches her budget by collecting end rolls of newsprint paper discarded after production at a local printing plant. The large sheets of paper lend themselves well to group activities, large flip charts, and many other uses. Wherever a newspaper is printed, a similar windfall of paper probably can be found.

A simple computer database that keeps track of training participants can increase your department's usefulness and credibility with department managers.

In the database, keep a record of training programs offered, participants who have completed each program and the date of completion, and the participant's department. On a quarterly, six-month, or prior-year basis, provide each department manager with a list of employees who have participated in training programs.

The report can:

• Give department managers a sense of the amount of training their staff members have received during the past reporting period.

• Keep department managers abreast of mandatory training completed or yet needed by their employees.

• Serve as a natural opportunity for you to communicate with department managers, to show appreciation for any support given, and to work cooperatively to find ways to improve how the training function supports them.

36

Enhance credibility by tracking participants' training histories

37

Planning cuts problems in coordinating off-site sessions

The benefits of holding a program away from the workplace are many. But with that decision comes new responsibility for making arrangements in an unfamiliar, and perhaps inconvenient, setting. These tips can help minimize confusion and reduce stress for the off-site trainer:

• Ship your program materials to a specific person. This step reduces the chance of the materials being misplaced in a remote location. Clearly mark them as 1 of 3, 2 of 3, etc. That way the on-site coordinator will know when all materials are received.

• Make sure someone at the training location brings copies of all hotel agreements. That way there is no argument about prior agreements with respect to arrangements for the meeting room, meeting room set-ups, breaks, and other provisions. It also ensures you have a list of specific contacts for various problems.

38

Advance planning keeps class disruptions to a minimum

A dvance planning will help limit interruptions of your training programs. You can minimize disruptions with these techniques recommended by Virginia Townsley, accounting department training administrator at Florida Power and Light Co.

• Offer programs off-site. Meeting in a hotel six blocks from the office diminishes interruptions.

• Hold all messages and then post them at breaks.

• Get advance support from management. The controller at Florida Power and Light once sent a memo to supervisors participating in a training course telling them they had 100 percent support from him and their managers to focus on the program. The memo also said they weren't expected to check in with the office during the two-and-a-half day program.

• Ask participants and their supervisors to practice the 500-mile rule — before making a call during a training program, have them ask themselves if they would call if the program were 500 miles from the office.

39

Make sure your training marketing grabs trainees' attention

Flyers, posters, memos, or other announcements of upcoming training programs make the all-important "first impression" to prospective attendees. The presentation on paper should be planned every bit as carefully as the training presentation in the classroom. Ask yourself these questions to ensure your course marketing is as professional as the program.

1. *Do you have a strong title?* Use of numerals helps to describe concrete benefits to attendees. "Supervision Fundamentals: 11 Strategies for Building High-Performing Work Teams," holds more promise than "Basics of Supervision."

2. *Are the materials attractive and readable?* Desktop publishing can make a program announcement look as though it's professionally typeset, and even the simple addition of press-type headlines can make a typewritten announcement stand out from the ordinary.

3. *Is the key question, "What's in it for me?" answered?* The sender, the participant, and payor should all be able to find somewhere within the announcement direct benefits the class holds for them.

4. *Is there a clear, strong program outline?* The program should

emphasize the practical knowledge trainees will be able to apply immediately.

5. *Are you using testimonials?* Testimonials not only from satisfied participants, but from their managers should be sought and incorporated into training publicity.

6. *Does the publicity indicate special features like extensive handouts and certificates?* All other things being equal, most people like "stuff."

7. *Does it feature short instructor biographies?* The instructor's credibility can be a big selling point, and it also provides the instructor with some recognition.

40

Resourceful scheduling encourages higher attendance

If staff shortages keep people from attending needed training sessions, try some creative scheduling alternatives.

Here are a few solutions:

• Schedule sessions so the minimum number of people from each department can attend.

• Schedule shorter, more frequent sessions so key people are absent from work areas for shorter periods.

• Encourage limited cross-training so staff can cover key responsibilities for employees who are being trained.

• Schedule training on employees' days off, after hours, or any time more convenient for employees.

• Split training between employee time and company time.

• Offer after-hours courses that allow spouses of employees enrolled to attend the courses free of charge.

• Offer a program communitywide through a local chamber of commerce. The additional registrations from the community can cover the cost of training materials and the trainer's salary, and recover some of the major cost of training to your company — employee salaries for attending sessions during work hours. This method also can have public relations value as a community service.

Guest speakers coming from outside your organization should not be left in the cold. When an outside speaker is a part of your training program, fill them in on as many details as possible.

• Ask the speaker to personally check the room set-up and audio-visual arrangements early enough to make any needed adjustments.

• Let speakers know you expect them to be available 15 minutes prior to a presentation and 15 minutes after.

• Give your audience a chance to interact with speakers after formal presentations by inviting the speakers to social hours, meals, or other activities.

41

Guest speakers should be well-versed in program details

42

Analyzing the costs of training clarifies important benefits

Is the training program you're about to develop worth the time, effort, and money involved? Here's a checklist of expense items to scrutinize when doing a cost/benefit analysis of training:

• Personnel costs for the program designers, support staff, subject-matter experts, and consultants.

• Material cost for participant manuals, instructor manuals, audiovisuals, etc.

• Travel and related expenses for course design and delivery.

• Training facility costs.

• Equipment costs — audiovisual equipment, computers, etc.

When analyzing the costs of these training elements, ask yourself:

(1) What would be the cost in lost knowledge and skills for the company to do no training at all? Will the money spent be worth the knowledge gained? (2) What are the training development costs? (You can comfortably add 20 percent to the estimate.) (3) What are the delivery costs? (4) Are there ways to lower costs on support staff or subject-matter experts without sacrificing quality? (5) Are there external reasons that training is necessary: cultural trends, legislation, company leadership, or workforce attitude?

There are few things more distracting to training participants' concentration than a presenter glancing at a watch or a wall clock. It makes them more conscious of time — Are we on time? Behind time? Near break time? Almost done? To remove the distraction, place a small clock with numerals at least one-half inch high behind your overhead program so it is visible to you but not your audience. As you make your presentation and change visuals, you can be constantly aware of the time without making it obvious to participants.

43

Remove distractions by using a small clock instead of a watch

44

Determine group size by intent of training activity

When designing projects, case studies, role-plays, and other activities, a common question is, "What size should the groups be?" The answer depends on what the trainer would like to accomplish by using a particular activity.

A group of two emphasizes teamwork and synergy and helps people see the value of multiple input, particularly if you alternate between working on one person's issue, problem, or challenge, and then the other's.

A group of three is the bare minimum for brainstorming, but one domineering person can overpower the two others in this situation. It is a useful arrangement, however, if you're using the triad training approach, in which one person assumes the role of mentor, the next the role of the mentoree or protégé, and the third person becomes the observer.

The protégé performs whatever task is required and then self-critiques what was done. The mentor then provides additional feedback based on observation. The observer's role is to provide feedback on how effectively the mentor coached or counseled. Each person cycles through all three roles. The benefits are three reviews of the material, each time from a slightly different perspective, which keeps interest up.

If you use triad training, consider expanding to a *group of four,* having all four rotate through the different roles. For example, if you chose to teach a certain skill, the protégé can teach the skill to the fourth participant as the learner.

Groups of five to seven are optimal for discussion purposes and brainstorming. They are large enough to generate a lot of discussion and ideas, but small enough so that the more timid participants don't get lost in the shuffle. A domineering participant is also more easily managed by this size group.

Any group larger than seven begins to lose its effectiveness for the purposes of group work.

45

Guidelines for selecting training meeting locations

Would any of us even know an ideal meeting room if we saw it (because most of us commonly have the experience of using less-than-ideal meeting situations)?

Here are some guidelines in evaluating a meeting room:

• *Convenience of location.* If you are running a multiple-day seminar, you may want the location away from the work site. Don't make it too convenient to run back to the office or down to the shop during a program break. You may never get your participants back. On the other hand, if you are running an hour-long session, give participants easy access to the site so there isn't grumbling about how much of a hassle it is to travel to "for only an hour."

• *Size and shape of room.* The ideal guideline is a 1-to-1.4 ratio. So, if a room is 20 feet wide, it ought to be 28 feet long. If you are using an overhead projector, and you intend to use a straight lecture-school style, you can get away with as little as 12 square feet per person. But if you want to promote participation and involvement, you'll need at least 25 square feet per person. So a 20 x 28 foot meeting room can accommodate roughly 23 participants.

• *Climate.* To keep participants awake and alert, 69 to 70 degrees is the ideal room temperature. Humidity should be kept around 50 percent.

• *Room lighting.* If you are using an overhead projector, is it possible to dim the lights over the projector screen in order to increase the visibility of visuals as they are projected? Can the lights be dimmed in certain sections of the room to improve screen visibility? Some lighting systems allow you to turn off every other bank of lights — but that's not necessarily a procedure that aids a presentation. You may need to run off the front bank of lights while leaving the rest of the room illuminated. You also don't want a room over-illuminated. Lighting levels should be set so glare is reduced and hard shadows are eliminated.

• *Noise levels.* If you are using hotel rooms for your training, ask for fixed rather than movable airwalls. If you find the noise level outside your meeting room unacceptable, and if you are unable to change to another room, try increasing the background noise within your meeting room in order to mask it.

46

Marketing tips breathe new life into programs

Programs often are introduced with little enthusiasm or promotional effort, and without much real promise of applicable benefits. If trainers post announcements like, "Basics of Supervision will be offered Sept. 27-28 in Conference Room A," why should anyone attend?

Line managers, with nothing more to go on than such a meager announcement, won't pay much attention.

Here are some examples of revisions that can breathe life into program announcements:

• Change "Basics of Supervision" to "Fundamentals of Supervision." It's belated to be talking basics to supervisors who feel they have already learned them. It's difficult, however, for people to argue with the importance of stressing management fundamentals.

• Change the entire course title to "Fundamentals of Supervision: 7 Strategies for Building High-Performance Work Groups." This promise is specific. Who can argue with the fact that all supervisors or managers would like to build high-performing work groups?

• Make available course objectives and complete course outlines.

Shawn Miller, quality coordinator for Eastman Kodak, Rochester, NY, sends a "prepack" of overview materials (including a quiz) to participants. The title page on the prepack reads: *Break this seal...read the information...answer the quiz...and win $$$.*

Participants who arrive with the completed quiz receive a $10 gift certificate. The prepack has a number of benefits, Miller says:

• It helps reduce training time by 45 minutes to an hour (the entire session is four hours) because trainees have already digested overview material usually covered in class.

• It places trainees on a common level of understanding of the material coming into the session.

• Doing the brief quiz exposes trainees to the basic material *twice* before arriving at training.

• It helps dispel learner anxiety by giving trainees background information so they feel more comfortable at the beginning of class.

Miller says he typically has an 80 to 90 percent response rate to the exercise. He often uses certificates to national stores like Sears or JC Penney, "because they can be spent anywhere by trainees if you are doing training on the road."

47

Incentive spurs trainees to complete pre-course work

48

Design programs for those who pay but don't attend

Running a great training program doesn't yield much satisfaction unless it's supported back on the job. Yet often training is viewed as an interruption to the job, not as an integral part of the job. How do we turn that around? Here are several suggestions:

1. *Make sure you design training for more than just the participant.* For training to be effectively supported, it must be designed for three groups of people — two of whom will not show up in the classroom. It must be designed for the sendor, sendee, and the payor.

You can't design for these three unless they're included in the process. Ask them (and others, as appropriate) what should be included in the course if it's to be practical, relevant, and useful to people on the job.

The sendor has to see that the employee will be more effective because of the training. What does this person need to know, feel, or do to be able to do his or her job faster, better, and easier? What are the benefits that I will gain or losses I will avoid, if I send this person?

The payor has to see that the dollars are well-spent to keep those dollars coming. And sometimes that means spending the dollars the way the payor thinks they should be spent. One training executive, who for three years had been fighting for every training dollar because his industry was in a down cycle, opted for a $10,000 increase in a new program design in order to include video. What he previously would have considered an unnecessary extravagance became a high priority because his executive vice president wanted to keep pace with competitors. If the payor wants video — and video is an appropriate method — then the payor should get video because that person's support is necessary for the training now and in the future.

2. *Get the sendor more involved in the program.* Send a list of course objectives prior to the course. Ask the sendor to check off the two or three that are most appropriate for the sendee. Ask the sendor to meet the sendee to go over the objectives, initial them, and have the sendee bring them to the first class.

After the course, have the sendee and sendor review the objectives, how the objectives were accomplished, and set up an action plan for implementing what has been learned.

49

Idea file is a ready source of creativity

Need to design a catchy cover for a guide or transparency and you're out of ideas? Drained of every ounce of creativity? An idea file can be a great way to get the creative wheels moving when you feel stumped, says Michelle Tomczyk.

She suggests keeping a file that includes photocopies of interesting book, manual, and magazine covers, training literature that catches your eye, and direct marketing that uses a fresh design approach. The evening news on TV — where background graphics are used to reinforce the spoken word — is also a great source for ideas. Tomczyk, project manager of instructional design at Automatic Data Processing Inc. in Parsippany, NJ, watches for interesting ways that type, layout, color, and shading are used to enhance the message, makes a note of the techniques, and puts them in her idea file.

Jan Timko, training and career development officer for the City of Mesa, AZ, markets her training through a bulletin prepared six times a year.

Her "Important News" training bulletin is distributed to all employees. Each page is set up for quick and easy references to information on training development opportunities, including a "Supervisor's Corner" on supervisor-oriented topics, and a "Spotlight" section that focuses on a new book, program, or videotape available in the organization's training library.

50

Special bulletin spotlights training classes

51

Trainees' comments can justify requests for audiovisual equipment

Pauline Williams, a development consultant for TDS Health Care Systems, uses participant comments to help justify expensive equipment purchases. She asks participants' permission to use positive comments from their evaluations, especially about equipment the department rents, as ammunition to support the purchase of equipment at a savings to the organization.

If participants really respond to your $90,000 video, consider quoting them to management. Capture their comments on your evaluation forms, get permission to use those comments, and you've bolstered your equipment purchase rationale, Williams says.

If you repeat the same program to different groups over several days, you've probably experienced the uncomfortable feeling of having passed this way before.

Eileen Keefe, research associate at CSR Inc., writes a master outline of all her activities, jokes, stories, visuals, instructions, and questions on a transparency. She doesn't project the outline for the class, but keeps it as a reusable checklist, and checks off each element as she uses it. That way she ensures she includes everything and avoids being redundant.

52

Reusable master outline avoids redundancies

53

Cutoff coupons expedite course registration

A course announcement format with a "cut off and return" coupon at the bottom simplifies registration paperwork for Sandra McKinney at the Higher Education Services Corp. of New York State. She has standardized all announcements into this simple memo format:

Sample Course Announcement

Paragraph #1: Course title, time, place, and qualifications needed to attend.

Paragraph #2: Course outline and objectives.

Paragraph #3: Special instructions, contact person, and phone number for questions.

- - - - - - - - - - - - - - -

Course Name
Filing Deadline
Return Address/Phone

Employee name/Title _____
Location/Phone # _____
Course date preferences _____
Supervisor's signature of approval ____

When preparing handouts for a course, consider providing a "bare-bones" outline of subjects to be covered, with plenty of space between items for participants to make notes. Mary Urzi, training officer for Wake County Social Services, Raleigh, NC, says the tactic maximizes a participant's interaction with the content and encourages retention. The outline also serves as a handy review sheet.

54

Bare-bones outline aids learning, retention

55

Alternative scheduling provides more attendance options

Increase attendance and personally involve participants even before a workshop begins by asking for their input on scheduling matters, says Bob Tomayko of Tom's Foods Inc.

Faced with the need to conduct one-day training programs on Saturdays, Tomayko decided to put the schedule to a vote. About a month before a workshop, he now mails a questionnaire to group members asking if they prefer a Saturday workshop or the "Friday night special," held after work.

Classes typically run five to six hours, and include a meal. As a further incentive, spouses are invited to attend the meeting and the dinner, or just the dinner. Participants say they appreciate the opportunity to bring spouses because it gets them more involved and helps the spouses understand their work.

"The use of alternative scheduling also lets us reach more people who need and want training," says Tomayko.

Who knows better than the people on the job what kind of training they need to do topnotch work? The in-house training program at Rudolph and Sletten Construction Firm thrives on the ideas it receives from employees.

Training director Thomas Kirkbride says people often ask, "Why don't we have a program on…" Kirkbride gives the interested employees a PIF (Project Initiation Form) to help them fully describe their ideas, and to help the training department make a decision on the suggested program. The form requests this information:

• Event Title/Objective: explain the reason for offering this workshop and what participants will gain from it.

• Audience/Major Subjects: attach topical outline, if possible.

• Format: seminar, lecture, conference.

• Length: number of hours, half day, whole day, etc.

• Possible Instructor(s): People inside or outside the company who could be discussion leaders, lecturers, subject-matter experts.

• Support Material: text, outlines, handouts.

• Number of Revisions Required — Shelf Life: annual, one-time, etc.

56

Tap employees for ideas on new programs, resources

57

Well-structured handouts inspire prolonged use

Overheads are beautiful, flip charts are great, games are dramatic, hands-on exercises are essential, but don't forget to put something in attendees' hands besides the yellow pad they have brought with them, says Charlotte Donaldson, education specialist at Newtrend, Orlando, FL.

Class handouts and workbooks are an instructor's best investment in class preparation time, she says. Donaldson always prepares a course outline and table of contents (combined for convenience), course objectives, topics with bulleted points to encourage good note taking, and a multitude of examples. Donaldson uses clip art graphics and desktop publishing to make the handouts more attractive

She recommends using lots of white space. "White space implies the class is covering a relatively simple topic, and that can help build learner confidence," she says.

Donaldson distributes handouts during the course (some to be added to workbooks), and color-codes them by topic. All handouts are hole-punched, which encourages participants to put all materials in their three-ring binder workbooks for future reference or review.

Computer trainers need to be prepared in case their mainframe or network system goes down during a session. How? Overhead transparencies can be an alternative to hands-on training at computer terminals, says Simira Tobias, employment service representative, EPD, Los Angeles.

When the computers *are* down, EPD's trainers write on prepared transparencies modeled after the various screens to simulate the hands-on technical training, filling in blanks with transparency markers. Enlarging the printouts makes for easier writing, she says.

58

Create alternative learning tools in case the unexpected occurs

59

Try organizing student handbooks by days, not topics

When you have a lot of handouts for a multiday course with several topics covered each day, set up student notebooks with tabs for each *day* rather than each *topic*, suggests Judy Betheil, creative writer with Avon Products, Newark, DE. Betheil puts a brightly colored page between each set of handouts behind each tab. The agenda then works as the table of contents. It's more convenient for the students, she says, and often less expensive, because fewer tabs are needed.

60

Training coordinator committee pools department resources

South Florida Water Management District, West Palm Beach, FL, a district employee development unit, uses a committee of training coordinators — one from each department to pool resources.

According to training director Arlene McClurg, "The training coordinators provide a single point of contact for each department, and they also help establish a pool of talent who are friends of training and will offer needed support."

She says the purpose of each training coordinator is to facilitate training in their departments by:

• Sharing innovative resources, ideas, policies.

• Processing requests for training.

• Attending monthly training meetings.

• Gathering training information to relay to departments.

• Serving as a feedback mechanism for the training staff.

• Assisting managers, supervisors, and employees in developing individual development plans.

• Advising training of needs in their departments.

61

Distributing handouts in unusual manner paces participants

Does this sound like a familiar problem? You have lots of handouts to be used in sequence during a session, and while you don't want people to read them ahead of time, you also don't want to take class time distributing them as each comes up.

Anne Closson, director of staff development for Fort Logan Central Health Center of Denver, suggests arranging packets in reverse order and placing the piles print side down around tables.

Ask participants not to touch the piles until instructed to do so. Before turning the first one over, ask participants if they've touched them, and hand out rewards to those who haven't. Closson says attendees get the idea not to race ahead or mix up the packets.

Often the hardest things to obtain become the most desirable and create the most interest, says Carol Pate from The Breakers, Palm Beach, FL. And playing hard-to-get is one way she successfully markets her training programs. Pate offers each course just enough times so there are always enough students left for one "hold-over" course the next month. Pate says the continual waiting lists make people anxious to get into the class, and those who do get enrolled feel privileged to have a spot.

62

Playing 'hard-to-get' is successful marketing ploy

63

Preparatory questions act as guide for presentation planning

To plan for presentations, Mary Ann Sayers, marketing manager at Coca-Cola in Don Mills, Ontario, asks herself the following questions:

• Does the opening message create awareness in the listeners' minds that there is a problem?

• Where do I want the presentation to lead participants? When I am finished with my presentation my attendees will (fill in the blank). Sayers suggests expressing this destination in terms of what "being there" will allow trainees to accomplish. She also asks, "Are my hidden agendas — business and personal — under control?"

• What assumptions did I make about my audience's desired destination? Can they get there from where they are now, or are my expectations too high for one presentation?

• Is what I'm trying to communicate a solution to my audience's problem? Does it answer their questions or benefit them? If they accept or believe this message will they be ready to take action? Does my message raise questions? Are the answers to those questions the main points of my presentation?

A planned seating arrangement that also divides attendees into small groups becomes more interesting when participants receive an intriguing advance notice, says Barbara Bellissimo, director of education and training for State Farm Insurance, Scarborough, Ontario.

She sends out a memo before her courses informing participants of their "team" name, which matches the course's subject matter. For example, for courses focusing on "problem solving," each table is given a detective's name, such as Sherlock Holmes or Dick Tracy.

The memo piques participants' interest, Bellissimo says, and also gives them the impression that the class will be not only informative, but fun.

64

Preclass intrigue piques trainee interest

65

Sending participants class photo stimulates post-course networking

To encourage post-class networking and reinforce training concepts, Pat Janssen schedules an extra-long break in classes that last more than five days. Janssen, administrator of purchasing education for John Deere Co. in Moline, IL, uses that time to take a group photo of her class. Two weeks after the class ends, she sends each participant a copy of the 8 x 10 inch photo, a certificate of completion and reminders about action plans they created in class. Class members are identified in the photo, and phone numbers are included to stimulate networking and sharing of post-training successes and failures.

For trainers who are "on the go" and do not have the luxury of a home base of operations or knowing what materials will be waiting for them to use at the training site, Ashley Fields recommends a "survival kit" of materials. All the items listed will fit into a copier paper-sized box or portable file box:

66

'Survival kit' keeps you prepared

Supply Checklist

Name tags	1 box of 50
Name "tent cards"	25-30
Transparency sheets	12
Sheet protectors (transparencies)	12
Dry erasure markers	1 box of 4
Flip-chart markers	1 box of 6
Black permanent markers	6
Pencils and pens	12 of each
Highlighters	12 (scented)
Masking tape	2 rolls
Overhead pens	1 box
Paper clips	1 box
Binder clips (to mount flip-chart sheets on walls with nails)	25-30
Post-it Notes	3 pads
Business cards	25-30
File folders (stuffed with 10 sheets of assorted, similar colored paper)	6
Scissors	1 each
Ruler	1 each
Note pad	1 each

67

Learning trainees' names, faces in advance adds personal touch

If you have access to photos of course attendees, Vicki Hampton, a training specialist with the Federal Bureau of Investigation, Los Angeles, recommends this technique for learning their names in advance of a training session and adding a personal touch to a course:

Write the name of each student on a course information packet and paperclip that person's photo (or a photocopy of the photo) to the cover. As you pass out the packets, use the photos to identify the recipients. Remove the photos before giving the information to the student.

68

Tips help eliminate typos in materials

Misspelled words — in course manuals or in notes on boards or flip charts you create during a session — can damage your credibility and make you appear unprofessional.

Ather Shabbar, assistant training manager for Sears Canada, Toronto, Ontario, provides these tips for avoiding embarrassing typos:

• When preparing printed materials, don't guess. If you don't know how to spell a word, look it up or ask an associate.

• Carefully proofread materials a day or so after completing them. Getting away from the text for a while will help you catch errors later. Again, enlist the help of an associate; the more eyes, the better.

• If you write extemporaneously during a session and come across a word you don't know how to spell, don't panic. Ask the participants for help. They'll perceive your request as honest, not unprofessional.

• Finally, if you have a typo, take advantage of the situation by adding a little humor. Lines like, "I believe a person is not very creative if he or she knows only one way to spell a word," or "This marker is defective; it can't spell," are good standbys.

69

Make mundane course information as lively as possible

To get through the mundane but necessary process of reviewing housekeeping information, Bob Schondelmeier, division training director for Marriott Health Care Food and Nutritional Services, Avon, CT, borrows a technique from *Late Night With David Letterman*. On flip-chart paper or overhead transparency, he lists the "Top 10 Most Frequently Asked Training Questions."

A sample list reads:

#10: Are we going to follow the agenda?

#9: Where are the bathrooms?

#8: When can I go home?

#7: What if I fall asleep?

#6: When's lunch?

#5: Do we get to take breaks?

#4: Where can we smoke?

#3: What if I get a message?

#2: Where are the phones?

#1: Who's paying for dinner?

Beginning with number 10, Schondelmeier provides the answer after revealing each question. The list can be easily customized, based on individual groups, he says.

70

Simple job aid eliminates cumbersome manuals

Bulky manuals designed to advise workers about new procedures or provide product information are often ignored or are too cumbersome for easy use, says Rosemary Durant. For that reason, she creates a more user-friendly version for typical computer procedures in her company. Durant, a senior trainer with Citadel Investor Service Center, Boston, takes certain core procedures — like step-by-step instructions for logging onto terminals — shrinks each step to 4 x 6 inch card size, laminates them, and then punches them for use in a Rolodex-like metal ring that can be easily accessed and flipped to certain steps. Trainees typically take the cards back to their job sites and use them as reference tools.

71

Sending training invitations by audiotape is unique approach

Most people have an audiocassette player in their office, car, home, or all three. So instead of sending the usual invitation to — or reminder of — training by memo or letter, Mike Redwood, a trainer with the W.R. Grace of Canada Ltd., Mississauga, Ontario, sends a tape of his voice.

The message can be easily recorded in your office, he says, and you can add your choice of music for background. With a dual cassette player and a minimal expense for blank tapes, you can then make the desired number of copies.

The tape, Redwood says, provides a great medium for letting participants know when and where the session will take place, what it has in store for them, and serves as an informal introduction of the trainer to those people who may not be familiar with him or her.

Prior to all sessions that involve employees from a variety of departments, Judi Hargreaves sends each participant a list of the other attendees, including names, departments, and phone numbers. Hargreaves, an assistant manager for the Canadian Imperial Bank of Commerce, Toronto, says the list eliminates the need for lengthy introductions at the outset of the course, provides trainees with a handy networking tool, and communicates to departments that other areas in the company have similar training needs.

72

Mailing a roster to trainees eliminates lengthy introductions

73

10 'don'ts' for classroom trainers

Jodi Todd, senior inside sales trainer with Microsoft Corp., Redmond, WA, offers a list of 10 "don'ts" for classroom trainers. Some of these warnings about personal appearance may sound like common sense, but others bring up points you may not have considered:

Don't...

1. Wear new or tight shoes. With a full day of training ahead, you'll be glad you didn't.
2. Forget to carry either breath mints or a toothbrush and toothpaste.
3. Wear hair accessories that need to be regularly adjusted or otherwise fiddled with.
4. Wear tight or restricting clothes. Be as comfortable as you professionally can.
5. Wear clanging jewelry that may be distracting.
6. Wear perfume or cologne that might be deemed "too strong."
7. Wear low-cut or potentially "risky" clothing.
8. Chew gum.
9. Wear controversial accessories like buttons with a political bent. Stay neutral.
10. Forget to bring your smile and enthusiasm to class with you.

Marisa Englund uses a simple piece of technology — an electronic "baby monitor" — to solve a problem created by teaching in classrooms without windows: When curriculum includes different instructors teaching portions of a class, there's no sure way to know when one is finished and another should enter the room. Englund, training coordinator for American Protective Services, Oakland, CA, wanted to ensure smoother transitions between class segments.

Englund's seminar design calls for interspersing guest speakers from different departments with the trainer's presentation. In a field supervisor's class, for example, a day includes a discussion of field supervision funds, and half-hour segments on sales, employee retention tactics, and workers compensation.

To eliminate distractions, she installs a baby monitor in the classroom, the kind parents put by infants' cribs. She puts the transmitter in an unobtrusive spot — usually behind a VCR — and places the receiver on her desk in a room around the corner to monitor course progress and make speaker transitions flow more smoothly.

74

Baby monitor ensures smooth hand-off between trainers

75

Mailing monthly course schedules speeds registration

Communicating course schedules to trainees at remote branches and getting timely enrollment responses is always an issue when operating a regional training facility, says Daniel Maselli, a training specialist at Northeast Savings, Hartford, CT.

He addresses this concern by sending a monthly mailing to each of 14 branch offices. The schedule is printed on legal-size colored paper. One side displays the training calendar on the upper half and the breakdown of courses on the lower half. The other side shows the company logo on the upper half, with the tear-off enrollment form below.

Because the schedule is only a single sheet of paper, it can be folded in half, stapled, addressed, and sent without an envelope. The enrollment portion can be returned in the same manner, because Maselli's name and address are printed on it.

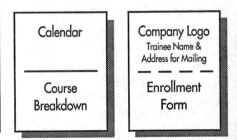

Section Two:
Needs Assessment Techniques

How do we make choices about what to include in a course? Here are several points to consider:

1. Ask people to separate their suggestions into *need to know* and *nice to know*. Need to know gets covered for sure. Nice to know gets covered if there's time.

2. Ask for distinctions between what people *need to know* versus what people *need to be able to find*. For example, there are typically five steps for dealing with an angry person taught in conflict management. When someone stomps into your office, slams a fist on your desk, and says, "I'm fed up. I'm not going to take it anymore," it's not a good time to say, "Excuse me," and reach into your desk for your course handout, thumb through it until you come to the right page, and say, "You seem upset. You need to know, and know right now."

3. Make sure what people need to find is in an easy-to-reference handout or manual. And make sure you spend time in class familiarizing them with that manual.

76

Guidelines
help
narrow
course
content
choices

77

Publications great sources of topic ideas, information

With content analysis a good rule of thumb is more information is better than less. It's much easier to boil down too much information than it is to expand or puff up too little. Here are a few tips on compiling information:

• Start with the past 12 issues of a half dozen or more publications that cover the concerns of the group you're addressing. Starting with the most current issues, list the topics covered and compare the list with topics covered 12 months ago, then 11 months ago, and so on. Exclude feature articles, which tend to be less immediately topical than columns and departments.

• As you list topics, also list the number of column inches devoted to each. Topics that may have received only a few inches of space four months ago are now receiving much more, and topics that were hot 10 months ago are receiving much less.

• Issues that demand the most space or have received increased attention in recent months will probably have the greatest stimulus for attendees at your next meeting, executive briefing, speech, etc.

• Now break down the broad topics qualitatively by reading the articles about the most promising topics.

While the principle reason for doing a needs assessment is to identify needs that can be met through training, assessment can have a political purpose as well.

Besides asking all of the questions you need to about whose input is needed from an educational standpoint, take time to ask whose input is needed from a political standpoint.

Consider questions like these:
• Who will benefit from the training? Survey them.
• Whose support will be needed for training to be used back on the job? Get their input.
• Who is most likely to resist? Find out why.

Training cannot be done in a vacuum. It requires input before and support after. Needs assessments can do a lot more for you than simply identifying needs.

78

Needs assessments can assist in getting managers' backing

79

Asking for managers' input can garner their support

There is no guarantee that the target group of a training needs assessment understands either the skills they need or the knowledge they lack to improve their job performance. Therefore, it makes sense to survey one level up (superior) and one level down (subordinates) from the members of the target group to make sure you really understand their needs.

This assessment technique can also sometimes have the added benefit of increasing buy-in and support for the training. If you ask employees one level up from your target group for their ideas — and if they see the results of the survey as identifying important deficiencies — you can look forward to greater support. Asking subordinates for suggestions increases the likelihood they will respond favorably to changes that take place in their environment as a result of the training.

An advisory committee is useful in conducting an effective needs analysis, but it can serve as much more than that. A well-chosen advisory committee can review your program as it is developed, be part of the group that experiences the "dry run," and it can use its internal credibility to help market the program throughout the company.

For example, a faculty team at Vanderbilt University developed an education forum for IBM's technical educators, one of the first steps taken was establishing an advisory committee composed of some of the most respected managers and trainers within IBM. The advisory committee had the following responsibilities: to review and comment on sites selected for field visits; review the suggested course outline and timetable for the two-week program; and attend a walk-through of the course 30 days before the first offering.

The input and credibility of the advisory committee contributed greatly to the success of the initial program and subsequent offerings. The committee (and key individual members) also helped smooth the way for class visits and interviews that had to be conducted on a very tight timetable.

80

Well-chosen advisory committees can answer many training needs

81

Checklist aids in ensuring assessment is accurate

How do you really determine training needs? There are a variety of methods. Here are a few:

1. Analyze the job.
2. Talk with the job-holders.
3. Analyze the problems.
4. Ask the supervisors of the job-holders.
5. Ask the subordinates of the job-holders.
6. Test the skills/knowledge of the job-holders.
7. Observe the job-holders performing the job.
8. Analyze past appraisals of the job-holders.
9. Form an advisory committee.

To make sure your assessments are accurate, use a combination of methods. One view may not be enough. For example, when a five-year management development plan for the New York State Department of Correctional Services was developed, the plan covered 5,000 supervisors and managers (more accurately called sergeants, lieutenants, and captains) in more than 50 correction facilities.

Working with an advisory committee (method 9) it was determined that methods 1 through 5, and number 7 would yield the needs analysis information needed. Interviews were conducted with the senior executives in the department and a site visit made to the Correctional Services Training Academy. Site visits were made to six correctional facilities: two low security, two medium security, and two high security. The senior executives — including the superintendent — in each facility participated in interviews. A cross-section of guards (or officers), sergeants, lieutenants, and captains also participated. Training records and promotion patterns were closely reviewed.

Based on the review of records and interviews, a survey was then developed that the supervisors, managers, and executives from all facilities completed and returned directly to assure confidentiality.

The result was a five-year plan that had buy-in at all levels of the organization. Equally as important was ensuring that the situation was examined from enough angles so that a clear picture of needs could emerge.

82

Study of performance problems should precede course

The attitude, "If all else fails, try training," can turn the training function into a scapegoat. It's critical for the training departments in companies with performance gaps to determine why that gap exists before leaping to provide training. Allison Rossett, professor of education and technology at San Diego State University, suggests four possible causes of performance gaps:

1. *Lack of skill or knowledge.* A gun to the heads of participants couldn't force them to perform because they lack the skills and familiarity needed.

2. *Environmental problems.* The copy machine is broken, critical raw materials are on back order, etc.

3. *Lack of incentive.* There's no reward, feedback, or consequence for doing, or not doing, what has to be done.

4. *Lack of motivation.* Employees either don't see the value of doing what needs to be done, or lack the confidence to do it.

The lesson? Training can impact factors 1 and 4, but is generally a waste of resources when used to address factors 2 and 3.

Every new group of participants brings a distinct set of needs to the classroom, so Bob Hunter, a trainer with Jostens in Minneapolis makes sure he has a good grasp of those needs before class ever begins. He sends prework questionnaires to all participants before his customer service training sessions, then uses their responses to tailor content where needed.

Some of the fill-in-the-blank questions Hunter sends to trainees — most of whom are customer service representatives — include:

Preclass surveys identify unique needs of incoming classes

Pre-Work Questionnaire Sample

• The people and events that increase demand (stress) on me in my role as a customer service representative are _____

• I know when I'm overstressed because (my early warning signals are) _____.

• The most difficult part of dealing with internal or external customers over the phone is _____.

• I feel most customer service representatives could improve their skills in these areas: _____.

• I will consider this program worthwhile if _____.

84

Analyze needs before, during, and after all programs

For your training to make a difference, you need to collect information at three key junctures of a program — before, during, and after the training takes place.

Before: Discover what the environment is like. What problems are training expected to solve, and who has identified those problems? If the learners have identified them, there will be more enthusiastic class participation because of the readily perceived needs. If it's the learners' boss or bosses, you can grease the skids for effective on-the-job, after-the-course support.

During: Do the participants see the ongoing training meeting their needs? Do the bosses see that the training is addressing issues they identified as important?

After: Do participants leave with specific action plans for applying their new skills and knowledge? Are bosses prepared to reinforce and allow time for the new skills to be reinforced on the job?

Will bosses hold participants accountable for using the new skills and knowledge? Is there an opportunity for each participant to block out time for skill practice to ensure on-the-job application?

With the understanding that trainees know best about their learning needs, Jill Livingston, director of training for Village Inn Restaurants, Denver, CO, asks for their input at the beginning of her three-day refresher classes for restaurant employees.

On day one she asks trainees to fill out index cards marked one, two, and three with answers to three questions listed on an overhead or flip chart: What is your best asset as an employee of this company? What would you like to learn, improve on, or be more effective at on the job? What can the company do to improve its operations? She also asks them to list years of experience in the restaurant business in the lower left corner, and number of years/months with her company in the lower right corner of each index card.

Recording that experience allows Livingston to show how she values drawing upon it during class.

She has participants fill out and drop the cards, unsigned, into a basket before lunch. The information allows her to tailor the next day's session, and also to "brag" on trainees' assets and how they can be used to improve peer learning.

85

Ask and ye shall receive: Trainees know their needs best

86

Five methods for observing skills of masterful performers

To analyze which skills and attributes distinguish "master performers" in specific jobs, consider these observation approaches:

1. *Direct observation.* Videotape and then review thoroughly.

2. *Task listing / task analysis by subject-matter experts.* A hierarchical listing of the performance standards of various jobs.

3. *Stimulus / response tables.* Construct a behavioral pattern of how a task or job is to be performed. Then observe the stimuli that generate actions or responses.

4. *Algorithms.* Build a precise set of instructions for solving a well-defined problem. Example: a car doesn't start. The first question: does the engine turn over? If no, at least part of the problem can be found in the electrical system. If yes, we can check for spark getting to the plugs, and continue on through a checklist in a precise sequence.

5. *Behavioral frequency.* Observe the number of times a behavior occurs to determine whether it has a positive, negative, or neutral effect on performance. Example: noting the quantity and types of verbal exchanges that occur while a customer service representative handles a customer complaint.

There's no need to be locked into your program agenda, even when it's based on a sound needs analysis. Here's a way to complete a needs analysis in class and ensure your agenda will cover the training needs of participants.

After a review of the program agenda, break participants into small groups of five to seven people. Ask the participants to identify additional topics that fall within the parameters of the programs they would like to discuss.

The technique offers the benefits of creating greater program ownership for participants, and of positioning the instructor as flexible and responsive to specific participant needs. The technique is best used when a program is a day or longer in length.

87

Incorporating participant input creates dynamic needs analysis

88

Group technique uses consensus for three-level assessment

The nominal group technique is a process that can be used for needs assessment at three levels: organizational analysis, operations analysis, or personal analysis. It can be used to get a working consensus from people interested in your particular problem or issue. By getting the right group of people together, you also can analyze an issue up and down the organization, horizontally across an organization, or even from organization to organization. You can also use it to have insiders assess an organization. Here are the seven steps to the nominal group technique:

Step 1. *Individual generation of needs, problems, tasks, and skills.* These are not to be collected. The items generated should answer a question and constitute a list.

Step 2. *Round-robin recording.* The facilitator records one item or need per person on flip-chart paper. (To make the process move faster, have volunteers record each category on separate flip charts.)

Step 3. *Item discussion.* Each item is discussed to make sure everybody understands it, and to allow for a discussion of pros and cons.

Step 4. *Number each item,* but only after all items have been discussed in Step 3.

Step 5. *Item importance.* Ask each participant to vote on the priority of the items. This can be done in a number of ways. You can use the "third plus one" rule. For example, if there are 24 items, one-third would be eight, plus one would be nine. Each participant would have nine votes to distribute among the 24 items. A second option would be to give each participant 100 points to be distributed in any proportion among the total number of items available. If they feel Item #3 is high in importance, they could assign it 50 points.

Step 6. *Review preliminary results.* Ask yourself these questions: Are the items selected realistic? How many of the high-priority items can be accomplished in a given timeframe? Are the resources and money needed available? Is it within the ability of the group to accomplish what is being recommended? Do any of the questions asked change our opinion about the order in which the items should be ranked? Do we have a working consensus among us?

Step 7. *The final vote.* If you have a working consensus in Step 6, tabluate, finalize, and distribute the results. Develop an action plan based on the recommendations.

89

Measuring performance in multiple ways breeds accuracy

Next time you're considering a needs analysis, keep in mind the concept of nonrepetitive redundant measures.

Simply explained, redundant means you are measuring the same thing, nonrepetitive means you're doing it in different ways. Why measure the same thing different ways? Because perceptions are not always accurate.

Asking a participant what his or her needs are may not get you the information you need to help improve their performance because the perception may be distorted. For example, if you ask a manager what skills she needs to improve, she might say giving feedback, delegating, and time management.

But that self-assessment is just one measure. In examining how both high- and low-performing managers spend their work time you may discover only insignificant differences. And since there is no difference you would want to avoid spending much training time devoted to the topic, although it does warrant being touched upon because it is a perceived need.

90

Start needs assessments by identifying problem causes

According to Alison Rossett, professor of educational technology at San Diego State University, a needs assessment begins with first identifying these four possible causes of the performance problem itself:

1. *Employees lack skill or knowledge.* Even if they want to, they don't know how to write purchase orders or operate the word processing program.

2. *The environment is in the way.* In other words, employees don't have the tools, forms, or work space to enable them to perform successfully. The classic example here is the computer that keeps going down.

3. *There are no, few, or improper incentives.* New policies and contracts for incentives, as well as training in their use for supervisors, are necessary.

4. *The employees are unmotivated.* Two related factors, value and efficacy, directly contribute to successfully motivating employees. Offer training that illustrates the benefits of quality performance and provides early, tangible success to build confidence.

91

**Survey
ensures
right
people
are in
pilot
programs**

When piloting a new course, Effie Rumsey, area manager of human resources at Southwestern Bell, San Antonio, TX, makes sure she has a feel for who should attend and what they will expect by surveying managers in advance.

She faxes each department manager a letter asking for a 15-minute appointment in the next several days to discuss the materials and the manager's involvement.

During the meeting she explains the course and asks the managers to deliver in person a questionnaire to 10 to 15 supervisors under them. The survey includes information about the class topic and dates, and asks supervisors to estimate the usefulness of the program to their staff. Rumsey uses the information to determine who needs the training most and to plan future scheduling needs.

U sing a network of affiliate councils to determine training needs can be effective in companies that have numerous sites with varied needs, says Chuck Thomsen, manager of education at Canada Trust, London, Ontario.

Canada Trust's regional affiliate councils, composed of a cross-section of management, including line managers, personnel directors, and upper management from each of the company's divisions meet twice yearly. They review current corporate training programs offered by the Canada Trust Management Institute, discuss proposed programs, and express their companies' training needs.

The chairpersons of the affiliate councils, called the "Dean's Council," also meet twice a year to discuss training concerns and needs of their regions. The meetings serve well in reviewing the beliefs, values, and commitments of the management institute, Thomsen says, and gives council members a broad understanding of new programs and policies.

The process allows line managers to have a hand in planning training, fostering grassroots support of the training and development effort, Thomsen says.

92

Involving managers in planning training fosters grassroots support

93

Market research can determine perception of training

To improve the selling of training to management, Karen Gates of Walt Disney World recommends doing market research homework to determine management's as well as business units' perceptions of training. Gates offers these guidelines:

1. Do a needs analysis (or gap analysis — speak the language of the business unit).

2. Conduct a customer survey.

3. Investigate the word-of-mouth reputation training has in the business unit.

4. Take a look at training statistics — how can you really demonstrate what you've accomplished with your training program? Next, review the research data you've come up with and create an action plan with short- and long-term goals. You may want to call this a "service level agreement" with customers.

5. Re-image the training department by changing the name. Don't, however, market "new and improved" if you're not ready to deliver.

6. Publish monthly, quarterly, and yearly training statistics, particularly if you want to make comparisons with prior years so people can see any improvement being made.

7. Be visible. Volunteer for com-

mittee assignments with your customers and business unit.

8. Include sessions on business processes in your management development classes like budgeting, purchasing, and employee relations.

9. Innovate. Become known as an idea person.

10. Integrate yourself as part of the business process/function. Don't become isolated. You're there to be a partner in helping to make things happen.

94

Look at realities, end-results to design effective training

To design and deliver training with impact, three things should be analyzed in the first steps of the design process. Try thinking of CR, ER, and WR.

1. What is the *current reality* (CR)? That is, what are the attitudes, skills, and knowledge levels the participants are going to bring with them to the program.

2. What are the desired *end results* (ER)? Look at what problems need to be solved through training or what skills need to be improved. Ask yourself: what are the expectations of managers and supervisors regarding their people once they have finished the training and what are the expectations of those who provide the budget?

3. What is the *workplace reality* (WR)? What factors exist in the workplace that indicate the proposed training may or may not be supported? This analysis is important in discovering what can be done to maximize factors that are likely to support the training and minimize those likely to keep the training from being used.

95

Performance, relevance both important in needs assessment

Almost every needs assessment deals with proficiency. But it is also important to focus on relevance. The next time you develop a needs assessment, consider using two rating scales. The first would rate the incumbent's performance in doing a job on a scale of one to five from extremely competent to no competence. Then rate the skills on relevance with the same scale, from extremely relevant to not relevant at all.

The ratings enable you to find out what competencies need to be developed by the individuals you design and deliver training for, and also helps you become aware of how important the various competencies are to the jobs performed.

The dual approach gives you useful information regarding how much time should be devoted to various areas in a training program, and whether certain areas need to be covered at all. It also helps you to examine whether skill practices may need to be built into a training session and to determine the information that could be delivered via a reference manual instead of class time.

96

Present training as last solution to most performance problems

Three words to remember for your next needs assessment are "*Should, Is, Cause,*" according to Goran Kindwall, a trainer with Wang Europe. In doing his needs assessment, Kindwall always asks job incumbents and supervisors three key questions: What *should* happen (ideally)? What *is* happening? What is the *cause* of the gap? The cause of the gap can then be analyzed to determine whether that need should be addressed through training or if there is another solution more appropriate to close the gap, such as a policy or systems change.

Two weeks before a workshop, Elizabeth Schiff, senior training manager for the American Academy of Ophthalmology, distributes a form she calls "Case in Point." The form asks registered attendees to describe problems they have encountered related to the course they will attend. Schiff then uses these cases for small-group problem-solving exercises (participants choose the group they want to join) or in role-play sessions.

Schiff says the "Case in Point" form gets participants thinking about the topic before they arrive and about how they might apply the workshop material to their own needs. The form also gives her advance warning of the types of issues her trainees are facing, allowing her to do advance research to be a more effective resource for participants.

97

Trainees' work problems best source for training case studies

98

What do you want from your participants: three main questions

To provide training of the highest quality, it helps to be aware of the three domains of learning: the cognitive domain (knowledge), the affective domain (feelings and attitudes), and the psychomotor domain (skills). These domains are best summed up by asking three questions about participants: What do we want them to know? How do we want them to feel? What do we want them to be able to do?

Making sure people acquire new knowledge is obviously a key component of training programs. There are six levels of knowledge to be aware of and test for during training:

• *The first level is simply wanting people to recall information.* Simple tasks that demonstrate participants are absorbing and remembering information include asking them to name or define a concept, answer who-what-where-and-when questions, answer yes or no questions, or to complete a describe, match, or select exercise.

• *The second knowledge level is comprehension.* To test for understanding we might ask participants to give an example, describe the consequences, explain the cause, compare how things are alike or different, or to paraphrase, summarize, or defend.

• *The third level is application.* People can demonstrate their knowledge by solving a problem, applying the principle, or by preparing, producing, or modifying the information.

• *The fourth level of knowledge is analysis.* At this level we want participants to be able to demonstrate their logical level of understanding. Tasks you might ask to be accomplished include identifying the reasons an author provides for reaching certain conclusions or to break down the steps in a given process.

• *The fifth knowledge level is synthesis.* We can gauge knowledge at this level by asking participants to create something new, combine previously learned elements, write a speech, create a diagram, develop a model.

• *The final level is evaluation.* Ask participants to make a judgment based on criteria, to give reasons for or against an argument, or to criticize, access, or appraise a situation.

99

Employees are valuable resources when revising programs

Ellen Rupert, training specialist for the New York State Thruway Authority, knows that employees who have already gone through a particular training session or already perform the task she must train others to perform are valuable resources when revising existing programs.

Rupert recently revised and expanded a toll collector training program, forming a work group of representatives currently involved with training or working in toll collection to recommend changes and strategies for the course. As content experts, Rupert says, they provided many valuable insights and ideas.

100

Surveying trainees links needs with course offerings

An annual needs assessment process called "Individual Development Plans" (IDPs) helps establish training goals for the year ahead and opens lines of communication between the training department and its customers, says Michael Dosch, marketing consultant with Northern States Power (NSP) in Minneapolis.

For example, to develop an IDP with sales, a training group representative meets individually with sales representatives and their managers to review the past year's training record, development goals, and areas for improvement for the coming year. The IDPs from all departments are coalesced into common topics, and the company-wide results lend themselves well to course content design. Dosch says the formal process of working through an IDP is also an excellent tool to use to communicate the need for and value of training to upper management.

101

'Town meetings' effective assessment tool for decentralized companies

As a decentralized company with offices in 34 cities, training needs analysis at Southwest Airlines is a challenge. But Liz Simmons, senior instructor of employee development with Southwest Airlines in Dallas, says the training staff addresses the issue by scheduling "town meetings" that give employees a chance to provide input on desired training.

The group of seven trainers divides up Southwest's hubs, and then each visits about five cities once a year to sit down with employees in an open forum and talk about what is and isn't working in training.

Simmons says the training department notifies the hub's manager, sets a convenient time, and publicizes the event through posters. The meetings typically last from 30 minutes to three hours.

The time and energy that go into town meetings are extremely well-spent, Simmons says. "Not only are we hearing first-hand from our customers about the challenges they face and what we can do and *are* doing to help them, but we're also staying in touch with the people interacting face-to-face with customers on a daily basis," she says.

About the Author...

Robert Pike has been developing and implementing training programs for business, industry, government, and other professions since 1969. As president of Creative Training Techniques International Inc., Resources for Organizations Inc., and The Resources Group Inc., he leads over 150 sessions each year on topics such as leadership, attitudes, motivation, communication, decision-making, problem-solving, personal and organizational effectiveness, conflict management, team-building, and managerial productivity.

More than 50,000 trainers have attended Pike's Creative Training Techniques workshops. As a consultant, he has worked with such organizations as American Express, Upjohn, Hallmark Cards Inc., IBM, PSE&G, Bally's Casino Resort, and Shell Oil. A member of the American Society for Training and Development (ASTD) since 1972, he has served on three of the organization's national design groups, and held office as director of special interest groups and as a member of the national board.

An outstanding speaker, Pike has been a presenter at regional and national conferences for ASTD and other organizations. He currently serves as co-chairman of the Professional Emphasis Groups for the National Speakers' Association. He was recently granted the professional designation of Certified Speaking Professional (CSP) by the NSA, an endorsement earned by only 170 of the organization's 3,800 members.

Pike is editor of Lakewood Publications' *Creative Training Techniques* newsletter, author of *The Creative Training Techniques Handbook*, and has contributed articles to *TRAINING Magazine*, *The Personnel Administrator*, and *Self-Development Journal*. He has been listed, since 1980, in *Who's Who in the Midwest* and is listed in *Who's Who in Finance and Industry*.

Want More Copies?

This and most other Lakewood books are available at special quantity discounts when purchased in bulk. For details write Lakewood Books, 50 South Ninth Street, Minneapolis, MN 55402. Call (800) 707-7769 or (612) 333-0471. Or fax (612) 340-4819. Visit our web page at www.lakewoodpub.com.

More on Training

Powerful Audiovisual Techniques: 101 Ideas to Increase the
Impact and Effectiveness of Your Training $14.95

Dynamic Openers & Energizers: 101 Tips and Tactics for
Enlivening Your Training Classroom $14.95

Optimizing Training Transfer: 101 Techniques for Improving
Training Retention and Application $14.95

Managing the Front-End of Training: 101 Ways to Analyze
Training Needs — And Get Results! $14.95

Motivating Your Trainees: 101 Proven Ways to Get Them to
Really Want to Learn $14.95

Creative Training Techniques Handbook: Tips, Tactics, and How-
To's for Delivering Effective Training, 2nd Edition $49.95

Creative Training Techniques Newsletter: Tips, Tactics, and
How-To's for Delivering Effective Training $ 99/12 issues